The cover design is from
Dora Dean or The East India Uncle
by Mrs. Mary J. Holmes
published by Hurst and Company, 1858

© 2012 by Gretta Vosper
ISBN 0-978-0-9737752-3-5

Published by File 14: PostPurğical Resources, Toronto, ON

We All Breathe

Poems + Prayers
by gretta vosper

We are an amazing family, we humans. Diverse in every aspect, we are yet strikingly similar. Our physical characteristics display variations on the typical – two eyes, arms, legs; ten toes and fingers; and a head crowned with hair of natural shades ranging from white through blonde, red, and brown to black. We thrive on the same nutrients delivered through an astonishing array of foods prepared in both ancient and ever more creative ways. We use the same parts of our brains, more or less, to explore radically different parts of our world and to engage in dramatically opposed and sometimes violently defended ideas. We all know joy, sorrow, exhilaration, and despair and we breathe our way – in and out – through them. Each one of us was born; each one of us will die. In between those two events, we all breathe.

For the past ten years, I and the congregation known as West Hill United have been on a very human but unique journey. Growing out of the Christian tradition, we've been exploring what it means to live in ways that honour our commonalities beyond the doctrinal and ideological beliefs that divide the human family. Gathering every Sunday morning to explore the terrain, we have learned much together and moved a considerable distance despite having to forge much of the path as we travelled. Some of the journey has been invigorating and breathtakingly beautiful. Some of it has been downright ugly. It has all been incredibly worthwhile.

Because the human family shares so many features and experiences, West Hill and I carry on with our task of creating community beyond the beliefs that divide with the hope that, within such communities, real dialogue can take place. Not surface dialogue. Not polite interfaith dialogue. Not rearrange the furniture dialogue. Real, let's-solve-these-problems-together dialogue. Because the human family has a lot of problems and it is going to take all of us to find the solutions. Even and especially when our differences threaten to divide us, we must remain true to the one often overlooked element that we each depend upon for our survival – love. Without it, all the clean air and water in the world, and all the best food on the planet is useless to us. In the end, I believe, it's the only thing that can ultimately save us.

Each of the following poems and prayers was written for use at West Hill in one of its gatherings. I offer them as invitations to the people in that community to explore new ways to love themselves, those around them, and the rest of the planet and those who share it with them. In so doing, we recognize and remember our interconnectedness. As we grow in love, making it deeper and more profound, we broaden our compassion and our willingness to embrace the diversity of life. That may not be what we first created religion to do, but I'm confident that, with or without religion, it is what we need to do now.

May this little collection offer wisdom for the journey.

Gretk

We all breathe.

From that first autonomous act,
to our final letting go,
we breathe our way
through every moment that is our life.

Deeply, as we prepare for enormous effort,
or a short, shallow pant
as we steer a course
through pain and fear,
our inhalations
pace the ecstasies of love,
and the tragedies of loss
binding exhilaration to sorrow
down the thread of our lives.

May we learn to breathe
not only days
but moments filled with joy.
And as we do,
may we remember long
that to breathe is to inspire.

Set in the corner,
three feet tall,
head bent,
outrageous act exposed,
we learned the difference between right and wrong.
Easy then, the line clear and well-defined;
"wrong is wrong" and "right is right"
divided the choices of our youth with simple precision.
But now, intricacies we do not understand
underscore our complicities
and the line has grown faint.
Where shall we set ourselves now,
bow our heads to pay our dues,
or is penance even possible?

May we welcome moments of reflection
that expose to us the truths of who we are,
not for the "strengthening of character" they might bring
but simply for our coming to know
the tangled wonder of our inner selves.
As those able to cherish
the unfolding moments of our lives, we pray,
Amen

Into our reflection,
we peer at who we are
and as we gaze at ourselves,
study the lines, colours, curves of our own faces,
we miss entirely who we really are.
It is as though a layer of imperfection
distorts the glass,
hiding our true selves
even from eyes yearning to see.
It is as though we are masked,
hidden within the projection
of what we should see.

May we learn to comprehend beyond
the transmissions of our optic nerves,
grow senses that might find us out
and touch, feel, listen for
the truths of who we are.
And when we find them,
may we wrap them once again,
in our own holiness,
in our love.
Amen

For some, the dance is essential,
movement spinning the self into a whole.
For others, music alone inspires,
harmonies resonating with the pulse in their veins.
Still others feel the weight of symbol,
drawing fragmented realities into one.
And the spoken word, poetry's elusive beauty,
commands the focus of yet other hearts.

Pause

Our needs are scattered
across the ribbon of preference, need, interest.
We hold to its purpose –
the inspiration of our souls.
May we ever seek to touch, engage, unite with
one another in the beauty of life
and the courage of love.
So may it be.

In a breath,
life comes to us,
drawing into us the world
and all we will know, experience, love.
In a breath, life leaves us,
our hopes, dreams, possibilities
exhaled into a vast and unknown eternity.
Breathe deep the residue of what has been.
Breathe deep the essence of what now is.
Breathe deep the elements coalescing into what will be.
All resides within us,
folded into us through the living we have done,
animating us in this moment of awareness,
lifting us toward tomorrow's light.
Breathe deep all of who we are and have been.
Breathe into all that we may become.
We breathe as those whose breath
yet calls us to tomorrow.
Amen

A settling, a soaring,
an arriving, a departing,
a question, an answer,
a stillness, a gesture...
our lives form in the in-between spaces
where what might happen
hasn't yet
and we are rulers
of what may become.
But we do not live there.
We live in the complexity
of decisions made,
choices taken,
words wrapped around silences
that should have been.
May we come to hold
the moments longer,
those within which our hearts are buoyed
and brought to deeper, truer meaning.
We bow as those caught in the mystery of life
yet holding all its variables
in our trembling hands.
Amen

held together by forces we've only begun to understand,
our world revolves around a blazing ball of fire.
from the distance,
it reflects borrowed rays
and its watery surface
shines a crystalline blue
into the great expanse of darkness we call
the universe.
closer,
we can see clouds, land, mountains, even.
but we cannot see borders.
may we,
whose national pride is dependent upon
invisible lines too often drawn and fortified by conflict,
ever seek to see beyond such lines
and come to honour and respect
all who live upon this planet
known to us all as home.
Into this possibility, we offer ourselves
as those who would have their lives
spin a persistent beauty
into a waiting world.
Amen

Our eyes turn toward the skies
as we are welcomed into hands,
cradled into folded arms
at the moment of our birth.
All we might be
awaits unfolding.
All we might create
has yet to coalesce.
All we might offer
lies dormant
in the unknown mystery of that perfect moment.
As we move through life
might we honour and celebrate
that moment of perhaps, of promise, of potential
in the lives of all we meet
aware that we are midwives of what might be
and are blessed by the constant training we receive
as we answer that high calling.
As those who create life throughout life,
we offer ourselves to this work.
So may it be.

We've turned ourselves
inside out and backwards
looking for the ultimate fix,
the great event,
the sale to end all sales
that will realize the
savings to end all savings
and make us happy.
We've built sandcastles,
country homes,
wilderness retreats,
and cottages by the lake—
all illusions of the perfect life that,
once we move in,
isn't quite what we expected.
Just beyond our reach
is the perfection we long for.
Do we keep stretching?
Or is it time to put our hands to other uses?
As those whose hearts must be ignited,
we dream.

It is through the simple things of life
that we are nourished.
In silence and celebration,
our spirits are nourished.
In contemplation and conversation,
our minds are nourished.
In relationship and solitude,
our hearts are nourished.
May we find in the simplicity of ritual
nourishment for the unfolding days
and may we sense connection
through the gifts we share.
As light into light, we pour ourselves,
May it be so.

Bow my head.
Set my feet parallel.
Cease the fidgeting.
Still the fussing.
Focus.
Focus on the stillness,
the ceaseless,
the set,
and the bowed.
Focus on self.
Focus on others.
Focus on hope.
Focus on love.
Amen

Beyond the traditions
we name as such –
the birthdays, anniversaries, Christmas Eves –
those times we pick up the past
and intentionally caress it,
in the moments of our ordinary days
or even those we ride out on the edge of possibility,
we live connected with what has passed away.
It reaches through the individuality of our lives
and holds us to rhythms, patterns, choices
that wrap us close
and comfort us,
easing our burdens in a chaotic world.
But the things of our past bind our hearts also
to what our minds know must be left behind
and we oft walk in confusion
among the remains of what has been.

When, in the bursting forth of a new day's truths,
we feel the unbinding of what once stood fast,
might we recognize the freedom upon which
we are invited to embark
and feel ourselves released
into a future of goodness, truth, and beauty.
We open ourselves to this possibility
with love for the ground upon which we walk
and the stars for which we reach.
Amen

Seeking recognition,
vying for attention,
calling out to be heard,
we design, assume, and accommodate ourselves to
patterns of behaviour
that bring us what we need.
We engage or sulk or entertain or disconnect,
often in an attempt
to heal a primary dissonance
deep within us.
Each of us lives out our familiar patterns,
over and again,
wearing them so smooth and easy
we often forget they are there.

In the effort to heal our world,
may we find in the easy patterns of our lives
all that keeps us
from a connection of integrity and truth
and seek to smooth it away,
reworking our substance to create ourselves anew.
And may we find, too,
all that reflects the truth of who we are,
honour the strength that protected it these many years,
and offer it, boldly and beautifully,
to a needful world.
This we offer as those upon whom the world waits.
Amen

An attempt,
a fallible attempt
at witnessing to what cannot be seen,
speaking of what cannot be heard,
capturing what cannot be touched.
A measure of wisdom
and another of possibility,
woven together,
creating story
that succeeds,
fails,
succeeds again
to inspire,
enlighten,
lift us.
Some call it truth.
Some call it poetry.
Some call it words, just words.
May we, as we sift through those things handed to us,
have the wisdom to discern
truths appropriate to our time and our lives,
and in the glare of their light,
see one another.
Really see one another.
May it be so.
May it ever be so.

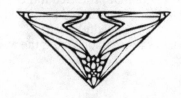

In the space between us
there must be a line
set between you and me
that keeps the ideas we have of one another
clear and constant.
There must be a line, too,
between before and now
and now and after,
and, no doubt, another one
that runs between those two.
And we should be able to find a line
between here and there,
between us and them,
between light and heavy,
cheap and too much,
beautiful and not bad.
And another line would be helpful
were it drawn between now and forever
but please, please, please
don't forget the one between
possible and impossible.
Without it, how will we know where to draw
all the other lines?
As those who clearly cross the line,
we offer ourselves beyond definition.
Amen

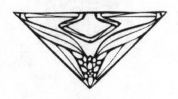

Decades of splendour,
richness, wealth,
spread thick around the globe
covering the stained and dreary
realities of life.
Far flung colonies,
wrapped in ideals not their own,
offered their beauty, their hopes, their lives.
May we ever be alert
to the presence we hold,
to the influence we wield,
to the damage we do,
so that we, who can see the world
only through our own eyes might see, too,
that its wonder is also beheld by those of others.
This we pray as we weave our own truth's
into tomorrow's folds.
Amen

Each finger a unique beauty,
the trace of light across it's tip
not replicated in other whorls of intricacy
anywhere else on the planet.
We are each wrapped wonder --
even the tissues that mould us
forming exquisite vessels for our complexities.
There is a dignity—often overlooked—
that resides in that diversity,
woven amidst the similarities we see.
May we choose to see
in eyes of different shapes, lines, and colours,
the inward beauty they depict
and in its myriad manifestations,
bow to the captivating power of life calling unto life.
This we pray as those captured within
                          and reaching beyond.

Amen

No careful placement,
no artful arrangement,
no idiosyncratic whimsy
could ever account
for the juxtaposition
of the strange and wonderful things in our lives –
laughter that erupts in the deepest moments of despair;
love that grows out of distrust and fear;
curiosity that ends in tragedy or delight.
Placed not only side by each
but dwelling within one another,
the events and realities of our lives
stun us with their incongruities,
with the intensity of their bizarre elements.
As we open ourselves to the mystery
that lies betwixt and between,
bewitched by its magic,
may our awe be magnified
and our commitment to discovery born anew.
This, we enter into,
as those born into wonder,
yet ever seeking it.
Amen

There comes a point,
when all has been given –
resources exhausted,
energy drained,
love spent.
Yet the body is built to move on,
seemingly unaware of its own limitations.
As though forged for another purpose,
it takes its rest and rises
to lift us into another day.
As the earth spins us into the light,
may we see in each new morning
both the things we love
and those we hate,
so that we might, again, push toward exhaustion,
aware that we are the creators of the world.
And as we fall away from light into darkness
may our rest be as gift,
the sweet repose of work well done,
the sabbath moments of tranquility.
As those whose dreams dance on a distant horizon,
we offer ourselves to the morrow.
Amen

Deep in the midst of all that I am,
is the rest of me –
not smaller,
not circumscribed by circumstance –
but bigger, by far, than most will ever see.
Bigger by far than who I know myself to be.
As I journey,
may I find opportunity
to come to know
this larger-than-life
who I am,
so that through my living,
I might learn
to love, embrace, and hallow me
and so free myself,
my real self,
to love, embrace, and hallow you.
As one who lives
to see and to be seen by you.
Amen

Stilled or stunned into silence
by the realities of life
to which we are exposed,
we feel our hearts open in response.
Stretched beyond simple, easy answers,
we are called,
through community,
to feel, experience, and engage
perspectives that rub against
the simplicities of our comfortable worldviews.
As we feel truths
score the tender tissues of our hearts,
may we recognize the work of love,
welcome its devastations upon us,
and rise, worthier still,
to carry its name.
As those born into love,
yet ever seeking it,
we risk its deepest truths.
Amen

We live in a world of surprise and beauty,
a world of colour and complexity,
a world of challenge and delight,
a world of anxiety and alleluias.
We are lifted and fed by the wonder in it,
humbled and laid low by its tragic realities.
In the interwoven moments of its blessing and blight,
we make our lives.
May we, in the spaces between sorrow and delight,
in the moments between harsh reality and beauty,
in the fear that lies in wait between truth and possibility,
learn the art of making light,
that we might shine with peace
and live with hope.
Together on this journey,
we share what comes
with dignity, grace, and love.
May it ever be so.

Inspired by the hands of hope
working, healing, holding, sustaining,
we gather this day to embrace
the task that is ours.
May our hearts
be strong for the work we find.
May our minds
be open to the challenges
it will provide us.
May our bodies
be ready when the call comes
so that no one is ever
left behind.
On this promise we stand
as those who see this world too clearly
and yet would see it
no other way.
Amen

Responsible for creating our every day,
we give thanks for the routines that offer us respite
from the thousands upon thousands
of decisions we'd need to make
were they not programmed into our psyches.
Carved from the lessons of our childhood,
sifted through our adolescent sensitivities,
placed one atop the other with adult precision,
they guide and shelter us,
save us from exposure
to the shifting, changing elements around us
and offer a permanence
we turn to in times of confusion and chaos.
May we be mindful of the strength
that lies in these pre-arranged stones,
aware that they point us
toward a home in.habit.ed
And may we ever be aware
of the roads that lead elsewhere,
roads we have not taken,
skies into which we have not risen,
nights into which we have not shone.
As those whose lives might mark the way for others,
we offer ourselves to the journey.
Amen

It is comfortable,
this place where my ideas have been tested,
my mind filled only with things I understand.
It is comfortable here,
where I know what I'm going to like/dislike,
choose to embrace/avoid.
It is comfortable
when I know all the answers
and can ignore whatever might challenge them.
It is comfortable when my opinions
are already formed/focused/prepared,
and I don't need to sort through different perspectives
and interpretations before I speak.

Yet the world moves,
spins at a catastrophic pace,
and I am forced into that small, fundamental space
between my comforts
and the gravitational force of truth.
May I find in the grip of such discomfort,
ideas/concepts/perspectives
that can draw me into a place not defined by comfort,
but the place, still, that I am meant to be.
As one who stumbles toward truth, I offer myself.
Amen

Wide, wide, was the opening road,
broad the way we undertook to travel.
Far above, swirling planets,
invisible in the brilliant light of day,
kept to their courses
as we travelled the easy, inviting way.
Their orbiting spheres
cast no shadows upon our quest
and, early on,
the harmonies of song lifted our hearts further still.

But day's light wanes
and trees close in upon us.
The way becomes cramped and uneven
and the points that could guide us
have been replaced by fear.

Comfort. Comfort.
Invitation.
Expectation.
Consolation.
Affirmation.
Slowly we make our way forward,
finally equipped.
Never alone.
As those whose solitude
strengthens solidarity,
we journey on.
Amen

It seems so far away and indistinct –
a horizon we can't imagine ever reaching.
And yet, here it is.
The future that once was
is now being lived out
amongst us.
We are the moments we shied away from.
We are the nightmares we let come true.
We're possibilities never envisioned.
We are promises we left unmet.
We are the freedom we took for granted.
We are the power we didn't grasp.
We are the courage we failed to muster.
We are the chances we never took.

We are the way we got here.
We are the future now.

We're also moments we'll yet walk into.
We're every dream that's yet to be.
We're possibilities that can still happen.
We're promises that we will keep.
We are the courage we'll need tomorrow.
We are the power yet to be claimed.
We are the freedom that we can offer.
We are chances we've yet to take.

We are the way we'll get there.
We are the future now.

Flickering lights
form themselves into images,
capturing lives
on the screen in front of us.
It's magic how that happens—
invisible waves
making their way toward my home,
pressing worlds I'll never know,
people I'll never meet,
through my walls
and onto the screen before me.
What am I offered by these fleeting images?
And how am I shaped, changed, challenged
by what they offer?
Wakeful dreams,
dreamlike reality,
shifting the centre
that is I.
As one who stares in a quest for beauty,
I pray.
Amen

Stirred by a yearning after goodness,
we scan our environs,
searching for signs of its presence
in what we find there.
In much, we find beauty;
in much, there is truth;
in neither is goodness bound to exist.
And so our quest is ongoing,
a constant assessing, filtering, and distilling
of what we encounter
and of what we gain.
May we ever be attentive
to those things that offer us goodness.
May it enter our hearts
and work to make us
vessels of the goodness
for which others seek.
As those who would offer
truth, beauty, and goodness,
we continue the quest.
Amen

It is not that you'd do anything differently.
It just happens.
You step into a moment,
open your heart,
and see your way forward.
Each moment of life unfolds
and offers up
possibility.
Nothing more.
It is yours to take and make of it what you will.
A squandering of hope?
The detritus of dreams?
A chain of broken promise
that tethers you to your past?
Or something else, something greater?
The grandeur of exponential beauty.
A torch lit by the incandescence of ideas.
Arms wrapped to hold, shield, protect, love.

Some call it heroism.
Some call it bravery.
Some call it sacrifice.
You call it living.

A stolen hour
and the night falls away
with such ease.
It cannot know the extra burden
its early retreat places upon us.
Days lengthen,
sunlight grows,
the sogginess of winter hangs about
teasing us as giant tears of former flurries
stream down our windowpanes.
Spring hesitates
and in the extra daylight hour,
we cast our gaze back
at what has been
and cast it forward
into what yet might be born
of the cold and dread of winter.
What has been the winter's take this year
and what, then, has it left us?
We persist as those whose questions call us on.
Amen

Upon turning the clocks forward an hour.

It is a wide sky
we huddle under,
each of us,
challenged by our birth,
to hold up our corner.

It is a deep sea
we wonder over,
each of us,
drawn by its beauty,
to care for it.

It is a broad land
we walk upon,
each of us,
marking our path,
must go lightly.

As we consider this Earth,
our home,
and we, our presence upon it,
may we be moved to see ourselves
as particles of the whole
and walk in reverence.

Into being the change, we move.
Amen

We shelter ourselves with images
of who we think we are—
intelligent and well-informed;
compassionate and well-intentioned—
until those wrenching, wild, chaotic moments
when we learn otherwise,
when life exposes us to glimpses of our otherselves—
intelligent but ill-informed;
compassionate but causing harm—
and we wish we could flee
from the complicities of our lives.
Into the lives of others,
we are bound to be woven.
Into the eyes of others,
we are compelled to look.
So it is we pray we may be
in the realities of others,
a gentle presence
that when we stand before them,
in utter, full disclosure of who we truly are,
we will not shy from the reflection in their eyes—
not the eyes of our children,
not the eyes of our partners,
not the eyes of our companions on the journey,
not the eyes of those we may never know.
As ones would see with a clear and honest vision,
we commit ourselves.
So may it be.

Darkness sits heavy on a broken dream.
Mere breath cannot heft its carcass
from the depths to which it falls.
It lies bereft of joys,
of possibilities,
of hope.
We turn our backs on it,
jaded,
and fold inward,
forget the chance we thought we had,
entertain ourselves beyond our misery,
convince ourselves we do not care.

Distracted, we forget the dream of what might be.
It lies safely entombed in the dank recesses,
locked in the realm of indifference, beyond our care.
Until, someone, somewhere,
touches a too-tender memory,
ignites something once alive,
something we know it would be easier to forget.

Possibility lifts again within us, building hope,
replacing the numbing pace of mere existence.
Exposed to the rich truth of our humanity,
we are, once again,
captivated by the dream of what might be.

And we awake.
We finally awake.

It is not as though
we stop and start our way through life,
jerking this way and that,
half yanking our feet from one course
and onto another.
It is not as though
we go so far and then,
consulting our maps,
make a sudden turn
and head off in a new direction.
It is not as though
we choose each new beginning
from a menu of life's options.
And yet
each moment opens soft and pure
awaiting our response;
each day lifts its head from the dew-strung grasses
and offers new hope, new possibility, extra chances;
each idea stirs a constellation of thoughts into being
and we are captivated by their courses.
May we know and celebrate new beginnings
in our lives and the lives of others
and as we do,
may we honour what has passed
and hallow its traces
through our lives, our hearts, our loves.
To this we commit ourselves
as those who begin anew this day.
Amen

A sky, streaked with the promise of day,
and I am called to anticipate all that might be.
The heat of the day heavy upon me,
and I am challenged to acknowledge
the responsibilities I hold.
The shade of the afternoon, like grace, soothes me,
and I am offered a reflection of my own rich gifts.
The cool of the evening
set in the midst of a candlelit heaven,
and I am awed by the fulfillment of another day.

We open ourselves as those who seek the holy.
Amen

Generosity.
Tenderness.
Innocence.
Sweetness.
Confidence.
Understanding.
Courage.
Compassion.
Eagerness.
She saw my sadness
and offered me her blankie.
May we each live with such gentle abundance.
So may it ever be.

How complex the world has become
and how brittle the language with which we describe it.
Each snowflake, each hibernating animal,
each step, each brain, each planet,
can be measured, weighed, examined.
So it is that we place them, carefully,
within our realm of knowledge.
Yet we yearn to find the meaning of them.
Beyond the tools we would use for examination,
may we seek out ways to contemplate,
to consider, to appreciate
each person, each thing, each moment
into which we come in contact.
And may the movement of our thoughts
from matter to meaning,
move not only our minds,
but our hearts to understanding.
As those who would celebrate beauty,
we seek its hidden sources.
Amen

In the centre of the whirlwind
lies an eye.
Still.
Open.
Calm.
Before we come into the world,
it is as though we live in that centre -
no worries,
no storms,
only peace.
As we find our way in life,
even in the midst of chaos,
may we remember that centre
and, as the need arises,
and it must,
may we hold
to the calm, open, stillness,
knowing it is home.
As those who walk the winds, we journey on.
Amen

Has anyone ever known?
Will anyone ever, ever know?

Were we to find ourselves lifted, in that moment of
death,
by a strength stronger than our own,
lifted to capture a vision of "it all",
to see the great events of life
laid out before us so that we might know—
the birth of newness,
the shining out of love,
the softening of rigidity,
the climax of met potential—
were we to see and understand all this,
would we strain to catch the breath that was our last
hold it, make it linger that we could see more,
or would the solving of mysteries
bring our need to engage to an end,
ease us away from what it was we have known
and move us, with calm, discerning assurance,
into what will be?

Look! Everywhere we turn,
in each intake of breath
and every word exhaled,
we dwell in possibility.
Our conscious realities intermingle
with worlds that are not known.
We flow toward that which is most precious to us
and through connection with it
are transformed, reworked, rejuvenated.
Even in our darkest moments
we are claimed by the truth of that unknown
and, ready or no,
pour ourselves into its ceaseless telling.
In that endless flow,
we become life itself.

May it ever be so.

Life—
urgent,
patient,
passionate,
composed—
we celebrate the myriad ways it comes to us
and we share it with others.
Through the voices of women who, down the ages,
have loved and lamented
the twists and turns of the lives of those they bore,
and the laughter and naïve impertinence
of their most innocent children,
we witness the beauty of life singing itself into being.
May we hallow life's gifts,
honour them in one another's lives
and find, wherever life pushes itself into being,
that which is sacred.
This we offer as life into life.
Amen

What incredible diversity exists in our world—
in nature, in our bodies, in our beliefs.
We live along the invisible line
that runs between
the "this" and "that" of our existence,
shifting our choices,
developing our ideas,
bending to the wisdom of those
whose perspectives we value.
May we ever seek and celebrate
the truths discovered along
a line illuminated by the best of who we are,
what we think,
what we value.
And may we hold one another to that line,
ever loving into the best of who we and they may be.
As those born into light,
yet ever seeking it...
Amen

We welcome the morning,
and as our world opens into daylight,
others shelter themselves in the coming twilight,
their world folding into darkness.
When we lift our hearts in celebration,
rejoicing in the beauty and wonder of life,
others offer up lament,
emptying their hearts of sorrow.
When we share the strength and courage of community,
others walk in isolation and fear.
May we ever be aware
that our realities are not universal
and so offer ourselves with humility
honouring the truths
in which our sisters and brothers live.
As those who would wrap this world in peace,
we commit ourselves.
May it be so.

Half of the sky,
held up by hands that are
creased with care,
smoothed with elegance,
lined with the effort of their labours,
closed in defiance,
open in generosity,
clasped in anticipation,
waving with joy,
bloodied by hatreds,
softened by love.
On this day,
as we celebrate and honour women,
may we remember the depths of their struggles,
and the breadth of their vision.
As those inspired by their persistent hope,
we reach toward that endless sky.
Amen

Since time immemorial,
we have gazed into the face of the universe,
its blind stare spilling back at us
from billions of suns, moons, stars.
Enriched by its mystery,
we cast into it our own—
stories of possibility, of hope, of promise.
As we have woven our days,
pulling and stretching
to match the sacred stories we had drawn,
too often the beauty of the myth
has risen far above
the realities with which we live.
May we find new stories in the skies.
May we sense new stories in our hearts.
May we write new stories on the stones of our world.
And as we do so,
may we pour the terrible beauty of truth
into ourselves and the world around us
so that those who come after us might find it there,
and live strong and powerfully
in its light.
We rise as those who seek to light truth's shining torch.
Amen

We live our lives with little regard
for the import of each moment.
They come to us
in regular and rapid succession,
and we live through each of them into the next.
A simple, ongoing process
into which our lives are set at birth
and through which we will proceed unto our deaths.
Yet in each moment resides incredible power—
new life,
healing,
opportunity,
and we, who move near-blindly through them
look to one another as we gather
that we may do together
the work of opening one another
to the truth of our potential.
May our singing be filled with transformation,
our words reflect the yearning of our hearts,
and the spirit that builds within us as we gather
hallow each and every passing moment
we know here together.
In expectation, we stand.
Open. Open. Open.

What are our darkest days,
stark of colour,
devoid of life?

What are our dull and listless moments,
in-betweens,
times spent waiting?

What is cold,
and emptiness,
and these tomblike spaces in our human hearts?

Against our darkest days,
light and celebration sparkle with wonder.
Alongside our dull and listless moments,
hope and action thrill our every nerve.
Into our cold and emptiness,
life pours beauty, love, a new day.

May the living of our days
ever place such moments side by side
that in the shelter of each other,
we might see each one as gift.

We set this vision before ourselves on this, the newest
day.
So may it be.

Tales of high intrigue,
of loves lost,
valour lived,
courage in the face of treachery,
justice at the very end
draw our attention,
covet our eyes.
We are fascinated by stories
that remind our imaginations
of emotions we once felt,
visions we once dreamt,
truths we once held up as essential,
yet let languish unattended
as we pursued other options.
Beneath the stories that thrill our hearts
lies a deeper narrative that,
true or not,
paves the road upon which we will walk.
May we feel the path beneath our feet,
be attentive to its direction,
and as we come to know its power
may we come also,
to know our own.
As those who would choose beyond the narrative,
we challenge ourselves.
May it be so.

Worlds waiting to be born, ripe with promise,
possibility,
purpose,
each wrapped in the watery reality
that is you
or I,
or another.
We enter into what has been,
craft it into what is and what will be,
and find our selves
amongst the messy landscape
of our creativity –
relationships begun and nurtured here,
half-formed truths growing there,
beauty bursting into bud between.
We create the realities within which we walk,
each seen and known and interpreted
as a completely different world
by someone else.
How strange the land that lies before us
when comprehended by
a different set of eyes
and how lost we are
in another's description
of the world we know and love.
As we settle into our comfortable selves,
may we ever be tuned
to the realities another walks amidst
and in so being,
grow a landscape drawn with love.
So may it be.

Since time began,
the mystery of death has captivated us.
Eluding our discovery,
we have wrapped it in stories and images
to help us cope with the reality of loss.
For some, the stories are of being reunited
with those they have loved,
being held again in a forgiving, reconciling embrace.
For some, the images take them
beyond the world as we know it,
cast them amongst the stars
to shine down upon those they have loved.
For some, they are scattered as molecules of energy
into the beyond that has wrapped them close
through the whole of their days.
Each seeks to trace a faint image
of a freedom we may know through death.
An opening.
A spilling forth....
We have ever yearned for answers,
longed to find the reason, the purpose, the truth of life.
We've plumbed the depths, ascended to the heights,
reached across innumerable barriers
to grasp what it might be
and still have found ourselves short of its full measure.
Yet we know it is here,
in the things that urge us forward,
that continue, beyond the opacity of thought,
to tantalize our questing, curious minds.
Who are we?
Why are we?

What you want.
No, what I want.
Maybe you'll want what it is I want
or I'll want what it is you want
or you'll just want for me what I want
or I'll just want for you what you want.
We can't stop wanting what we want
but maybe we can trim it down a bit,
share...
or something like that.

Step into your choice
as I step into mine.
Open your senses
to every miniscule change within you.
Open your heart
to the senses we've yet to name.
Feel where your choice takes you.
Do you feel bigger?
Can you see farther?
Was it right?

We do not live by bread alone.
Yet what is it that sustains us
in this place beyond yet within the confines of our
bodies?
What feeds our spirits,
stirs our hearts,
makes our blood pound
for reasons far more than physical?
Is it meaning,
the quest for meaning,
that sets our feet upon the floor
to search within another day?
Is it delight,
the joy of resting
at the furthest edge of wakefulness
in the warm caress of the memories
woven of a lovely day?
Is it love
rinsing clean every painful hurt,
every worry
with its "honey, I'm home!" relief?
Is it you?
Is it me?
Is it us?

is my lens wide enough
to take in the beauty, the desecration
the complexity and simplicity
the regular and the extraordinary...
is my lens wide enough
to capture diversity, random movement
patterns of exquisite correlation ...
is my lens wide enough
to sense shadow and depth
purpose and passion
dependence and autonomy ...
is my lens wide enough
to know the difference
between right and wrong
curved and circular
straight and narrow ...
is my lens wide enough
to see you and me
the distance between us
the ideas that might separate us forever ...

may our perspective
shift and change
stretch and expand
open and inform.
as those too often captured
by a too narrow lens,
we pray,
amen

An eternity of thanksgiving
and still the world
would turn and turn
into new beginnings,
new beauty,
new wonder.
Perhaps no end
to gratitude,
to hearts stilled in amazement,
to breath stopped by wonder,
to minds sparked by possibility.

But we –
whose hearts beat in staid, sedate, and steady rhythm,
whose breath is measured, unengaged,
whose minds are numbed by the length of our days –
we could starve for lack of inspiration.

May we feel the rush of time before us
approaching with a fierce, irreversible zeal.
May we boldly open our arms,
stand naked before its turbulent truth,
and know that it is all we ever have to lose.

Then, with hearts caught
in wonder, grace, and gratitude,
may we dance in time's furious passing
and learn to love the dance.
So may it be.

Wrapped
in the mystery of what is,
standing on the history of what has been,
unprepared for the whatevers that will come our way,
we fidget and fuss
with the routines of our everyday realities
making little dramas of our what to wears
and who said what about no one we know anyway.
We are captivated by what presents itself as real.
It keeps our eyes locked on what we can see,
our hands reaching only for what can be
touched, weighed, measured,
our ears dulled to anything outside a certain range –
the never-ending cacophony
of what it is we've labelled "life".
What is real blinds us to what is really real.
We don't see,
and most of the time,
we don't even want to.

But once in awhile, a too long while,
it shimmers across our vision,
rustles over top of someone's voice
or underneath the TV drone,
sets itself, lighter than air, upon our skin
and we sense rather than see, hear, feel
a moment's awareness.
Aware of us or we of it,
the moment is gone too quickly for us to really know.
May we ever be open to such moments
and when they arrive,
celebrate the sense of gift with which they leave us
and leave the analysis of fact to someone else
as we rest in the lingering beauty of the moment.
This we enter into
as those who would choose to lose themselves
in the richness of such moments.
So may it be this day.

Perfectly ordinary ...
It was perfectly ordinary.
Until you arrived.
And you.
And you.
And I am stretched beyond
what might have been,
beyond the quiet simplicity of my space
and into the oft chaotic world
of compromise and possibility,
cooperation, expectation.
With you.
And you.
And, of course, you.

May we cherish
each intertwining moment
and see within it
all the complexities,
wonders,
delights
of relationship.
So may it be.

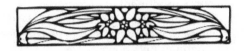

Nothing is clear.
Even the present moment
is sifted through those long since gone,
our reactions
only ever the products
of moments and experiences
we no longer remember.
Disentangling the threads,
undoing the knots,
finding the sources,
these things help
but we remain limited in our discernment,
unable to blink our way
to the clarity we desire.
May we find,
in the tumble toward tomorrow,
a firm ground to land upon
and a softness in the landing
that greets us –
not as those with no history,
but as those who hold it with reverence
as we walk into an unfolding world.
Amen

Whisked through the motions of a morning service,
we have scarce enough moments to capture our thoughts
and the time together is through,
our commitment to one another
reflected upon, strengthened, renewed.
But what of that gnawing seed of discomfort
that sometimes puts down roots, unbidden,
and carries me to the edges of despair?
Where is its place in our time together?

In our need for affirmation,
for energy,
for our passion to be good,
is there room for when we are not,
for when we fail,
miss the mark,
deceive,
and devalue?

In our coming together,
may we find the openness we need
to be truthful with one another
to expose the whole of who we are
to the light of understanding
that we might come to know
not only those who share the pews with us
but our very selves.
As those who would brave the truths of who we are,
we stand before one another.
Open. Open. Open.

It only makes sense
(when you think about it)
that we've evolved from some previous form,
its own function defined and confined
by its capacities,
its contexts,
its world.
It only makes sense
(when you think about it)
that being stuck where it was
wasn't enough,
its wings spreading,
feet strengthening,
back shifting to upright.
It only makes sense
(when you think about it)
that we aren't finished either
but only half through becoming
what it is we might become.
But it is hard to think about it
in the midst of life,
boggled as we are by its complexities.
May we find the space, the permission, the time,
to open our minds to an evolutionary extrapolation and
(when we're ready)
imagine ourselves in flight.
As those confined but not defined
by our physical realities,
we stretch toward an unknown future.
Amen

Easter Week

How beautiful the energy of those ignited by a dream!
How filled with song and dance and passion!
They set their sights on points of possibility
and work, play, inch, leap, edge, sing themselves,
(and often those about them)
toward their far-off summits,
ever-over-brimming
with the joy of what will be.
May we catch the awe
that sweeps up their hearts
and casts them toward a more beautiful tomorrow!
May we fill our arms with all their world will need!
And may we hear,
even in our darkest moments,
the hope they beat into our hearts with their passage.
May it draw us into harmony,
filling us with a passion all our own.
This we breathe into being,
as those who dwell in possibility.
Amen

So easy.
It would be so easy
if we were but given something,
...anything...
that might tell us clearly –
not in signs and symbols
but right out there, in black and white –
what it is we are here to do, to be, to offer –
what life is all about.
Maybe a list.
Maybe a map.
Maybe a crystal ball!

We have but stories of what has been,
tales of what was wanted and did not turn out,
ideas of what might make things better,
what might fill the husks of daily life
and make them swell with a wealth of meaning.

May the story of this week
inspire us in ways that bring us a hope-filled clarity
about who we are, what we can do,
what it is our lives might be about.
And as we walk this dusty path,
may we see only
the love and passion of those who journey with us
and be inspired.
Amen

Into the spaces left
where dreams once wove their hypnotic beauty,
spills first emptiness, sorrow, shock, despair.
We shrink from the realities
that have shattered our possibilities
and flee the fragmented truths whose edges,
honed to lethal sharpness,
threaten to destroy us, too.

But light seeps in.
Even on the run, we are caught in its dispassionate glow.
And though it cares not what we do,
as we emerge from shadowed roads of mourning,
it seems to bear a hallowed energy
– life –
and calls it to us,
to those who follow after,
and sets into our hearts another dream.

In all our places of loss and loneliness,
all our moments of fear and despair,
may we open our hearts to life
as it comes to us this day –
borne on a light-filled morn.
Amen

This light which bathes the world,
pours from a source so close, so near
and yet we cannot touch it
or fence it in that it not be lost.

This light which shatters darkness
is pieced together, flame by flame,
shining from a thousand sources
but is diminished by the loss of one.

This light which fills the furthest corner
brings with it warmth
to fill billions of hearts
and bind them with its common truth.

This light which pulls us toward tomorrow
is carried deep within each of our hearts
and lit by you and me and him and her
and all who live upon this earth.

This light which is yours and mine to carry
burns only in the hope-filled heart,
the source of all our inspiration
and all the beauty that will ever come to be.
Let it shine.

Thanksgiving

Encased in the stuff of "who we are"—
labels, collections, memories, things –
our movements are sluggish, laboured.
We believe we move with fluid sweeps through space,
but we are deceived,
for we bump and jostle our way through life
encumbered by our extremes,
unwittingly disturbing, destroying, and dehumanizing
as we beat our way along the path of prosperity.
As we seek to express gratitude
on this day of thanksgiving,
may we recognize the burdens
we have nestled in beside our blessings
and commit ourselves to lifting our hearts free
of those things that lessen all of us.
In the light of beauty we walk.
May it be for us the light of truth.
Amen

Expectation,
blazing from our minds
like a movie projector—
it casts before us
the brilliance of the day we hope to have.
Larger than life,
its fabled glow
measures our moments
and we stand small and silent
'neath its gloried shadows.
How can we match its splendor?

On this day of thanksgiving,
may we shut the lamp of expectation,
still the ceaseless yearning after perfection,
let the film of "what should be" run off the reel
and gently slip, forgotten, to the floor.
Then,
as eyes accustom to the sacred beauty of what is,
might we find our truest blessings
and give thanks.
As those whose hearts brim over with gratitude,
we open ourselves to these gifts.
Amen

Advent

We've always been waiting.
Waiting for life to finally begin.
Waiting to grow up.
Waiting to get out of here.
Waiting for our ship to come in.
Waiting for the right guy, the right girl,
the right somebody.
Waiting for another chance.
Waiting for the next shoe to drop.
Waiting for a smile.
Waiting for someone to know who we really are.
We've always been waiting.

In the moments, minutes, hours, days, years that we
have, then –
the time between now and whatever is waiting to happen
–
let's have a *good* time
and make it rich and beautiful
for all.

Into and out of these waiting times,
we weave our lives.
Amen

Winter

Spun into a velvet darkness,
we greet this midwinter night.
Promises of wonder, delight, and hope,
lie waiting for us to capture them
and make them real,
building a world that shimmers with beauty.
Into the moments between
receiving and giving,
may we weave a tapestry of celebration;
and as we cherish the gifts it has to offer,
might the beauty, truth, and goodness
that resides within us all
be illumined with new meaning for each of us.
May the world spin this night into wonder.
As those born into love,
yet ever seeking it,
we offer ourselves to the quest.
Amen

Wrapped in the frost of a winter's morn,
the world around us glistens with latent promise.
Beneath the dried and frozen twigs
buried in the soft earth,
lie the warm days of summer –
the greens of the meadows and fields,
the moving, invisible life forms
that feed on what is left behind
and make it into what will one day be.

What lies beneath those parts of us
we could describe as "dried and frozen" –
hearts too old and tired to care,
routines too easy and comfortable to change,
ideas we defend long past their prime?

In the dormant days of winter.
inspired by nature's silent, invisible work,
may we find ourselves reaching for transformation.
May we find ourselves.
As those whose shadows pace our lives, we wait.
Amen

Snowbanks, windshield wipers, frozen fingers...
winter folds around us, creeps into our joints
and slows us down.
That's what winter is for,
if you can believe it -
closing in our world,
shuttering the windows,
stopping life in its tracks
so that the journey loops back on itself
and can start once again.
Back at the beginning.
Back into the promise that lies,
wrapped by a filmy membrane,
in each exquisitely configured cell.
Back into the darkness
whence the deepest dreams come.
Back, sheltered in the fertile ground
sown with endless possibilities.
Back to the morning of a waiting world.
In this season of slowdown and icicles,
may we sense the wonder of what might yet be
and find ourselves at the centre of it.
In amazement, we stand.
Amen